# VODKA
## *Cocktails*

# VODKA
## *Cocktails*

More than 40 recipes for
delicious drinks to fix at home

Photography by **ALEX LUCK**

RYLAND PETERS & SMALL
LONDON • NEW YORK

**Senior Designer** Toni Kay
**Editorial Director** Julia Charles
**Head of Production**
 Patricia Harrington
**Art Director** Leslie Harrington
**Publisher** Cindy Richards

**Drinks Stylist** Lorna Brash
**Prop Stylist** Luis Peral
**Indexer** Vanessa Bird

First published in 2021 by
Ryland Peters & Small
20–21 Jockey's Fields
London WC1R 4BW
and
341 E 116th Street
New York, 10029
www.rylandpeters.com

10 9 8 7 6 5 4 3 2 1

Recipe collection compiled
by Julia Charles. Text copyright ©
Julia Charles, Ursula Ferrigno, Laura
Gladwin, Louise Pickford, Ben Reed,
William Yeoward. Design and photographs
copyright © Ryland Peters & Small 2021

The publisher wishes to thank Tom Dixon
www.tomdixon.net for the loan of
glassware used in the photography.

ISBN: 978-1-78879-379-7

A CIP record for this book is available from
the British Library. US Library of Congress
CIP data has been applied for.

Printed in China

FSC
www.fsc.org
MIX
Paper from
responsible sources
FSC® C008047

# *Contents*

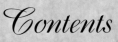

Introduction    6

BRUNCH COCKTAILS  8

CLASSIC SIPPERS  22

SUMMER COOLERS  34

AFTER DARK  50

Index & Credits  64

# Introduction

Vodka makes the ideal base for a cocktail and is perhaps the most useful spirit to have in your home bar. Its clean and neutral taste pairs well with plenty of other drinks ingredients, from tangy juices to sweet liqueurs, and provides delicious possibilities for every drinking occasion. This perfect collection of recipes showcases all the most popular vodka drinks, plus offers up some new surprises, and is a celebration of the cocktail in its myriad forms. The recipe methods themselves are easy to follow and require just a few pieces of basic bar equipment. You will need a cocktail shaker and a measuring jigger and will find a small sieve/strainer useful, as well as a stirrer or long-handled barspoon. A wooden 'muddler' can be useful for crushing fruit in the base of a glass or shaker, but the end of a wooden rolling pin will work just as well. Some cocktails are stirred rather than shaken, and this is done in a mixing glass or jug/pitcher or the cup/ beaker part of your shaker. As far as glassware is concerned, rocks glasses are useful and wine glasses can be good all-rounders but coupes, flutes and Martini glasses, in particular, will always give a more polished presentation. Enjoy garnishing your creations, too, and make them even more enticing with citrus slices, fresh berries and edible flowers, and, if the style of drink calls for it, add attractive drinking straws. And lastly, ice, you'll need plenty of ice! All of the recipes will require ice for both preparation and serving, so stock up on ice trays and make ice in batches so you always have a ready supply. Whether it's for a special occasion or just for fun, making a vodka cocktail is always going to be time well spent!

# BRUNCH
# COCKTAILS

# Sea Breeze

THE SEA BREEZE IS A MORE MODERN, THIRST-QUENCHING
VARIATION ON THE CLASSIC SCREWDRIVER (SEE PAGE 36).
THE CRANBERRY JUICE ADDS A LIGHT, FRUITY, REFRESHING
QUALITY AND COMBINES WITH THE BITTER GRAPEFRUIT
JUICE, MAKING IT VERY POPULAR WITH PEOPLE WHO
DON'T PARTICULARLY ENJOY THE TASTE OF ALCOHOL.

50 ml/1²⁄₃ oz. vodka
150 ml/5 oz. cranberry juice
50 ml/1²⁄₃ oz. fresh grapefruit juice
a lime wedge, to garnish

## Serves 1

Pour the vodka into a highball glass filled
with ice cubes. Add the cranberry juice and
top up with the grapefruit juice. Garnish
with a lime wedge and serve.

# Bloody Mary

THIS RECIPE FOR THE ULTIMATE BRUNCH DRINK PEPS THINGS UP WITH LIME JUICE AND A SMOKED SALT RIM ON THE GLASS.

500 ml/2 cups tomato juice
a few dashes of Worcestershire sauce
a few dashes of Tabasco hot sauce
salt and freshly ground black pepper
smoked salt flakes, to rim the glasses
15 ml/½ oz. freshly squeezed lime juice
100 ml/3⅓ oz. vodka
celery stalks and lime wedges, to serve

*Serves 2*

Put the tomato juice in a jug/pitcher. Stir in the Worcestershire sauce and Tabasco. Season with salt and pepper and chill for 30 minutes. Put the salt flakes on a plate, dip the rims of 2 glasses in water and then into the salt. To serve, add the lime juice and vodka to the seasoned tomato juice and stir well. Fill each glass with ice cubes, pour in the drink, finish each with a celery stalk and lime wedge and serve.

# Prosecco Mary

TRY THIS ELEGANTLY SIMPLE VARIATION OF THE BLOODY MARY (SEE ABOVE), WITH A LITTLE OPTIONAL HINT OF SMOKINESS.

30 ml/1 oz. vodka
75 ml/3 oz. tomato juice
a dash of Tabasco hot sauce
a pinch of sugar
¼ tsp smoked water (optional)
about 75 ml/3 oz. chilled Prosecco
cucumber ribbons, to garnish

*Serves 1*

Pour the vodka, tomato juice, Tabasco, sugar and smoked water (if liked), into a cocktail shaker half-filled with ice cubes. Shake vigorously and pour into a flute or rocks glass. Add half the Prosecco and stir gently to combine. Top up with the rest of the Prosecco, add some cucumber ribbons down the side of the glass and serve.

**NOTE:** Use a vegetable peeler to make the cucumber ribbon garnish.

# French Martini

THIS SIMPLE THREE-INGREDIENT COCKTAIL IS GREAT FOR BRUNCH PARTIES AND PAIRS SWEET RASPBERRIES WITH TART PINEAPPLE. SHAKE HARD AND YOU WILL BE REWARDED WITH A FLUFFY WHITE FROTH ON THE SURFACE OF YOUR DRINK.

50 ml/1²/₃ oz. vodka
10 ml/¹/₃ oz. Chambord
   (black raspberry liqueur)
75 ml/3 oz. fresh pineapple juice
pineapple wedges, to garnish (optional)

## Serves 1

Pour all the ingredients into a cocktail shaker filled with ice cubes. Shake sharply and strain into a frosted Martini glass or coupe. Garnish with pineapple wedges on a pick (if liked) and serve.

# La Dolce Vita

THEY DON'T CALL THIS DELICIOUS COCKTAIL LA DOLCE VITA ('THE GOOD LIFE') FOR NOTHING. IT MAKES A BRILLIANTLY FRESH AND LIGHT ACCOMPANIMENT TO ANY BRUNCH DISH.

**about 8 small seedless white grapes**

**1 tsp clear, runny honey**

**30 ml/1 oz. vodka**

**chilled Prosecco, to top up**

**a lemon zest, to garnish**

*Serves 1*

Put 5 of the grapes in a cocktail shaker with the honey and muddle well until they release their juice. Add the vodka and half-fill the shaker with ice cubes. Shake vigorously and strain into a chilled Martini glass. Top up with Prosecco, garnish with the 3 reserved grapes and a lemon zest on a pick, and serve.

# Elderflower Cup

ADD SOME SPARKLE TO A CELEBRATORY BRUNCH WITH THIS REFRESHING COMBINATION OF ELDERFLOWER LIQUEUR AND PROSECCO. THE FLOWER GARNISH ADDS A PRETTY TOUCH.

**20 ml/²/₃ oz. St. Germain Elderflower Liqueur, or elderflower cordial for a lighter drink**

**60 ml/2 oz. vodka**

**1 tsp freshly squeezed lemon juice**

**chilled Prosecco, to top up**

**edible flowers, such as violas, to garnish (optional)**

*Serves 2*

Combine the St. Germain (or cordial), vodka and lemon juice in a cocktail shaker. Add a handful of ice cubes and shake until frosted. Strain into 2 tumblers and slowly top up with chilled Prosecco. Garnish each with a few edible flowers (if liked) and serve.

# Bay Breeze

PINEAPPLE ADDS A TROPICAL TOUCH TO THIS VARIATION
ON A SEA BREEZE (SEE PAGE 9). OMIT THE PINEAPPLE JUICE,
DOUBLE THE CRANBERRY AND ADD A LIME WEDGE FOR
A CAPE CODDER (SEE PICTURE ON PAGE 8).

60 ml/2 oz. vodka
45 ml/1½ oz. cranberry juice
75 ml/2½ oz. fresh pineapple juice
chilled soda water, to top up (optional)
pineapple wedge and leaf, to garnish

*Serves 1*

Combine all the ingredients in a
mixing glass filled with ice cubes.
Stir to chill and pour into a highball
glass filled with fresh ice cubes. Top
up with a splash of soda for a lighter
drink (if liked). Garnish with a
pineapple wedge and leaf and serve.

# Pineapple Sangria

THIS PERFECT PITCHER DRINK IS LOOSELY BASED ON A
SPANISH SANGRIA, IN THAT IT COMBINES WINE WITH FRUIT
AND A SPIRIT BASE, IN THIS CASE TASTY PINEAPPLE VODKA.

1 x 750-ml bottle fruity white wine
200 ml/6½ oz. Smirnoff Pineapple Vodka
250 ml/1 cup fresh pineapple juice
125 ml/½ cup fresh orange juice, strained
about 250 ml/1 cup chilled soda water
lime slices, to garnish

*Serves 6*

Combine the wine, vodka,
pineapple juice and orange juice
in a jug/pitcher and stir. Top up
with the soda water and stir again.
Pour into ice-filled rocks glasses
or tumblers, garnish each glass
with a lime slice and serve.

# Prima Donna

SIMPLY COMBINE A ZESTY ITALIAN LEMON LIQUEUR WITH VODKA, TANGY POMEGRANATE JUICE AND CHILLED ITALIAN SPARKLING WINE, FOR AN ELEGANT AND PRETTY DRINK.

25 ml/³/₄ oz. vodka

15 ml/¹/₂ oz. Limoncello
   (Italian lemon liqueur)

25 ml/³/₄ oz. pomegranate juice

chilled Prosecco, to top up

pomegranate seeds, to garnish
   (optional)

## Serves 1

Put the vodka, limoncello and pomegranate juice in a cocktail shaker and add a handful of ice cubes. Shake sharply and strain into an ice-filled rocks glass or tumbler. Top up with Prosecco and serve.

# Peach Blossom Spring

THIS IS A SLIGHT DEVIATION FROM THE CLASSIC BELLINI,
WITH A LITTLE EXTRA KICK FROM VODKA AND PEACH LIQUEUR.
PERFECT SERVED AS A SOPHISTICATED DRINK WITH BRUNCH.

30 ml/1 oz. vodka

30 ml/1 oz. peach purée

10 ml/¹/₃ oz. crème de pêche
  (peach liqueur)

chilled Prosecco, to top up

2 dashes of peach bitters

a fresh peach slice and a mint leaf,
  to garnish

### Serves 1

Add the vodka, peach purée and
crème de pêche to a cocktail shaker
filled with ice cubes and shake to
mix. Strain into a flute glass and top
up with Prosecco. Add 2 dashes of
peach bitters, garnish with a peach
slice and a mint leaf and serve.

# Blackberry Bellini

A CLASSIC VENETIAN BELLINI IS A COCKTAIL MADE WITH
WHITE PEACH PURÉE PAIRED WITH PROSECCO, BUT THE SOUR-
SWEETNESS OF RIPE BLACKBERRIES WORKS BEAUTIFULLY HERE.

5 fresh blackberries

1 tsp white sugar

30 ml/1 oz. vodka

2 tsp freshly squeezed lemon juice

chilled Prosecco, to top up

### Serves 1

Put 4 blackberries and the sugar in
a cocktail shaker and gently muddle
until pulped. Add the vodka and
lemon juice to the shaker with a
handful of ice cubes and shake until
frosted. Strain into a flute, top up
with Prosecco, garnish with the
remaining blackberry and serve.

# CLASSIC SIPPERS

## Passion Star Martini

THIS CROWD-PLEASING COMBINATION OF VANILLA
VODKA AND PASSIONFRUIT HAS SPREAD FAR FROM
ITS ORIGINS IN THE EARLY 2000S TO BE ADOPTED
(AND ADAPTED) BY BARS THE WORLD OVER AND
HAS CERTAINLY BECOME THE STAR OF THE SHOW!

1 ripe passionfruit

30 ml/1 oz. vanilla vodka

15 ml/$\frac{1}{2}$ oz. Passoã
(passionfruit liqueur)

$\frac{1}{2}$ tbsp freshly squeezed lime juice

$\frac{1}{2}$ tbsp sugar syrup

chilled Prosecco, to top up

## Serves 1

Halve the passionfruit and scoop the
seeds into a cocktail shaker. Add the
vodka, Passoã, lime juice and sugar
syrup. Add a handful of ice cubes and
shake vigorously. Strain into a Martini
glass or coupe and top up with Prosecco.
Garnish with the other half of the
passion fruit and serve.

# Vodka Martini

PERHAPS THE MOST ICONIC OF ALL APERITIFS, THIS ELEGANT DRINK IS PERFECT FOR ANY CLASSY OCCASION.

15 ml/$^{1}/_{2}$ oz. dry vermouth

75 ml/2$^{1}/_{2}$ oz. vodka

a lemon zest twist

2 unstuffed green olives on a pick, to garnish

*Serves 1*

Put a Martini glass in the freezer to frost. Pour the vermouth and vodka over ice cubes in a mixing glass. Stir slowly to make the cocktail very cold. Strain into the chilled Martini glass. Hold the lemon zest over the glass and twist to spray a fine mist of its oils onto the cocktail. Discard the zest, garnish the drink with the olives on a pick and serve.

# Lemon Drop

CRISP AND REFRESHING, THIS CITRUSY COCKTAIL PROVIDES A TANGY TREAT. SERVE AS AN APERITIF BEFORE LUNCH.

about 1 tbsp caster/superfine sugar

finely grated zest of 1 lemon

25 ml/$^{3}/_{4}$ oz. freshly squeezed lemon juice

50 ml/1$^{2}/_{3}$ oz. vodka

25 ml/$^{3}/_{4}$ oz. triple sec

*Serves 1*

Mix the sugar and lemon zest on a small plate. Take a chilled Martini glass and dip it into water and then into the sugar and zest mixture to rim the glass. Pour the lemon juice, vodka and triple sec into a cocktail shaker, add a handful of ice cubes and shake vigorously. Strain into the prepared glass and serve.

# Classic Cosmopolitan

THIS PUNCHY, SWEET AND SOUR COCKTAIL IS HUGELY POPULAR FOR A REASON. THE CRANBERRY JUICE IS JUST THERE TO ADD A SOFT PINK HUE AND MAKES THIS THE PERFECT PARTY DRINK.

35 ml/1¼ oz. lemon vodka
20 ml/⅔ oz. triple sec
20 ml/⅔ oz. freshly squeezed lime juice
25 ml/1 oz. cranberry juice
a flamed orange zest, to garnish
   (see page 60)

*Serves 1*

Add all the ingredients to a cocktail shaker filled with ice cubes, shake sharply and strain into a chilled Martini glass. Garnish with a flamed orange zest and serve.

# Metropolitan

THIS COCKTAIL IS A FRUITY VARIATION ON THE COSMOPOLITAN (SEE ABOVE), USING BLACKCURRANT VODKA, COMBINED WITH THE CRANBERRY AND LIME JUICES.

35 ml/1¼ oz. Absolut Kurant Vodka
20 ml/⅔ oz. triple sec
20 ml/⅔ oz. freshly squeezed lime juice
25 ml/¾ oz. cranberry juice
a sprig of fresh cranberries and
   a lime zest, to garnish (optional)

*Serves 1*

Combine all the ingredients in a cocktail shaker and add a handful of ice cubes. Shake sharply and strain into a chilled Martini glass. Garnish with a small sprig of fresh cranberries and a lime zest (if liked) and serve.

# Appletini

CRISP, TART AND DELICIOUS, THIS VARIATION ON A VODKA
MARTINI (SEE PAGE 24) MAKES A DELICIOUS ALTERNATIVE.

45 ml/1$^1$/$_2$ oz. vodka

25 ml/$^3$/$_4$ oz. freshly squeezed
lemon juice

20 ml/$^2$/$_3$ oz. sour apple liqueur
or green apple schnapps

25 ml/$^3$/$_4$ oz. sugar syrup

green apple slice or fan, to garnish

*Serves 1*

Add all the ingredients to a cocktail
shaker with a handful of ice cubes.
Shake vigorously and strain into
a chilled Martini glass. Garnish with
an apple slice or fan and serve.

# Polish Martini

THE BITTERNESS OF ZUBROWKA AND THE POTENT
SWEETNESS OF KRUPNIK (BOTH POLISH VODKAS) COMBINE
WITH THE APPLE TO CREATE A BEGUILING DEPTH OF TASTE.

25 ml/$^3$/$_4$ oz. Krupnik Vodka

25 ml/$^3$/$_4$ oz. Zubrowka Bison Grass
Vodka

25 ml/$^3$/$_4$ oz. cloudy apple juice/
soft apple cider

*Serves 1*

Pour the 2 vodkas and the apple juice/
soft apple cider into a mixing glass filled
with ice cubes. Stir until chilled, strain
into a chilled Martini glass and serve.

# Legend

INVENTED IN LONDON IN THE LATE 1980S BY LEGENDARY
BARTENDER DICK BRADSELL, THIS RECIPE SHOULD BE
FOLLOWED CLOSELY, AS TOO MUCH OF ANY INGREDIENT
CAN RESULT IN AN UNPALATABLE COCKTAIL...

50 ml/1²⁄₃ oz. vodka

25 ml/³⁄₄ oz. crème de mure
   (blackberry liqueur)

25 ml/³⁄₄ oz. freshly squeezed lime juice

a dash of sugar syrup

a lime or lemon zest, to garnish

*Serves 1*

Add all the ingredients to a cocktail
shaker filled with ice cubes, shake
sharply and strain into a chilled
Martini glass. Garnish with a lime
or lemon zest and serve.

# Metropolis

PERHAPS INSPIRED BY THE PARISIAN CAFÉ SCENE CLASSIC,
THE KIR ROYALE, THIS DRINK COMBINES FRENCH SPARKLING
WINE WITH THE SAME APPEALING BERRY NOTES BUT ADDS
A KICK OF VODKA TO GIVE IT A STEELY EDGE.

25 ml/³⁄₄ oz. vodka

25 ml/³⁄₄ oz. crème de framboise
   (raspberry liqueur)

chilled Crémant, or other dry sparkling
   white wine, to top up

*Serves 1*

Combine the vodka and the crème
de framboise in a cocktail shaker
and add a handful of ice cubes.
Shake until frosted and strain
into a Martini glass. Top up with
Crémant and serve.

# Raspberry Martini

THIS LOVELY SWEET AND FRUITY MARTINI IS QUITE THICK IN CONSISTENCY BUT IT SHOULD STILL FLOW EASILY OUT OF THE GLASS.

50 ml/1$^2$/$_3$ oz. vodka
a dash of crème de framboise
  (raspberry liqueur)
dash of orange bitters
15 ml/$^1$/$_2$ oz. raspberry purée
fresh raspberries and a lime slice,
  to garnish

*Serves 1*

Shake all the ingredients in a cocktail shaker filled with ice cubes and strain into a chilled Martini glass. Garnish with raspberries and a lime slice and serve.

# Breakfast Martini

NOT ACTUALLY RECOMMENDED TO ACCOMPANY YOUR BOWL OF CEREAL, UNLESS EARLY MORNING IS ACTUALLY LAST THING AT NIGHT FOR YOU... BUT THIS CITRUSY DELIGHT IS DELICIOUS AT ANY OTHER TIME OF THE DAY.

50 ml/1$^2$/$_3$ oz. vodka
2 tsp Seville orange marmalade
an orange zest, to garnish (optional)

*Serves 1*

Pour the vodka into a cocktail shaker and add a handful of ice cubes. Add the marmalade and shake sharply. Strain into a chilled Martini glass, garnish with an orange zest (if liked) and serve.

# SUMMER COOLERS

# Purple Haze

THIS COOLER IS A LONGER, SPARKLING, SUMMER SERVE OF THE POPULAR PURPLE HAZE SHOT. TO MAKE SHOTS, SIMPLY MIX EQUAL PARTS OF VODKA, CHAMBORD AND LIME JUICE AND DIVIDE BETWEEN CHILLED SHOT GLASSES.

45 ml/1$\frac{1}{2}$ oz. vodka

30 ml/1 oz. Chambord
(black raspberry liqueur)

chilled lime soda or sparkling
clear lemonade, to top up

fresh raspberries, lime wedges
and mint leaves, to garnish

## Serves 1

Pour the vodka and Chambord into a cocktail shaker and add a handful of ice cubes. Shake well and strain into an ice-filled rocks glass. Top up with lime soda or lemonade, garnish with raspberries and mint leaves and serve.

# Harvey Wallbanger

THE HARVEY WALLBANGER IS A SPIN ON THE SCREWDRIVER
(SEE BELOW) WITH THE ADDITION OF GALLIANO, A UNIQUE
ITALIAN LIQUEUR WITH HERBAL AND VANILLA NOTES. IT ADDS
SWEETNESS AND ALSO CREATES A NOTABLY DIFFERENT TASTE.

**50 ml/1²/₃ oz. vodka**

**15 ml/¹/₂ oz. Galliano Liqueur**

**freshly squeezed orange juice,
to top up**

**an orange slice or large strip of zest
and a cocktail cherry, to garnish**

Build the ingredients over ice cubes in
a highball glass and stir. Garnish with
an orange slice or zest and a cocktail
cherry on a pick and serve.

*Serves 1*

# Screwdriver

THIS IS SUCH A SIMPLE COCKTAIL SO USE A GOOD VODKA,
FRESHLY SQUEEZE YOUR ORANGE JUICE AND KEEP BOTH
WELL-CHILLED BEFORE MIXING YOUR DRINK.

**45 ml/1¹/₂ oz. vodka**

**freshly squeezed orange juice,
to top up**

**a few dashes of Angostura or
grapefruit bitters (optional)**

**an orange slice, to garnish**

Fill a highball or rocks glass with ice
cubes, then add the vodka. Top up
with orange juice, add a few dashes
of bitters (if liked) and stir. Garnish
with an orange slice and serve.

*Serves 1*

# Moscow Mule

GINGER BEER IS WHAT GIVES A MULE ITS EASY SPICINESS AND IT WORKS BEAUTIFULLY HERE WITH ZESTY LIME TO CREATE THE PERFECT REFRESHMENT FOR A HOT SUMMER'S DAY.

50 ml/1²/₃ oz. vodka
1 lime, quartered
chilled spicy ginger beer, to top up

*Serves 1*

Add the vodka to a copper tankard or highball glass filled with crushed ice. Squeeze over the lime wedges and drop the spent husks in too. Top up with ginger beer, stir gently and serve.


# Strawberry Mule

BREAK THE ICE WITH THIS FRUITIER VERSION OF THE CLASSIC MOSCOW MULE (SEE ABOVE).

2 thin slices of peeled fresh ginger
4 fresh strawberries
50 ml/1²/₃ oz. vodka
15 ml/¹/₂ oz. crème de fraise de bois (strawberry liqueur)
a dash of sugar syrup
chilled spicy ginger beer, to top up
a lime zest, to garnish

*Serves 1*

Put the fresh ginger and 3 strawberries in a cocktail shaker and crush with a muddler. Add the vodka, crème de fraise and sugar syrup. Add a handful of ice cubes, shake sharply and strain into an ice-filled highball glass. Top up with ginger beer and stir gently. Garnish with the remaining strawberry and a lime zest and serve.

# Sgroppino

SERVE THIS DELICIOUS VENETIAN CLASSIC AS A REFRESHINGLY
LIGHT DESSERT, PERHAPS AFTER AN AL FRESCO LUNCH?

30 ml/1 oz. vodka

4 scoops lemon sorbet

15 ml/$^{1}/_{2}$ oz. single/light cream

90 ml/3 oz. chilled Prosecco

finely sliced or grated lemon zest,
to garnish

## Serves 2

Put the vodka and a small metal mixing
bowl in the freezer for a few hours before
you prepare the drink. Add the vodka,
sorbet, cream and Prosecco to the chilled
bowl and beat with a small whisk until
combined, light and foamy.

Divide the mixture between 2 flutes or
coupes. Sprinkle a little lemon zest over
each and serve.

# Sparkling Cosmopolitan

THIS IS A FUN TWIST ON THE CLASSIC COSMOPOLITAN (SEE PAGE 27). THE ADDITION OF SPARKLING PROSECCO TURNS IT INTO A LONGER MORE REFRESHING DRINK, IDEAL FOR SUMMER GATHERINGS.

45 ml/1½ oz. vodka
15 ml/½ oz. triple sec
15 ml/½ oz. freshly squeezed lime juice
15 ml/½ oz. cranberry juice
chilled Prosecco, to top up
a lime slice and fresh cranberries
　　(optional), to garnish

*Serves 1*

Combine the vodka, triple sec, lime juice and cranberry juice in a cocktail shaker and add a handful of ice cubes. Shake until chilled. Pour into a rocks glass or tumbler and carefully top up with Prosecco. Garnish with a lime slice and a few fresh cranberries (if liked) and serve.

# Cosmo Royale

FOR A LUXE SPIN, ADD A FLOAT OF CHAMPAGNE. THE BUBBLES WILL HAPPILY SIT ON THE SURFACE IF YOU POUR THEM GENTLY!

35 ml/1¼ oz. lemon vodka
15 ml/½ oz. freshly squeezed lime juice
15 ml/½ oz. Cointreau
25 ml/1 oz. cranberry juice
chilled Champagne, to float
an orange zest, to garnish

*Serves 1*

Add all the ingredients, except the Champagne, to a cocktail shaker filled with ice cubes. Shake sharply and strain into a chilled Martini glass. Gently float the Champagne on the surface, garnish with an orange zest and serve.

# Raspberry Lime Rickey

THIS IS A LIGHT COCKTAIL THAT IS BOTH FRESH AND FRUITY, WITH A SWEET TASTE OF RASPBERRIES AND A HINT OF LIME.

**6 fresh raspberries**

**50 ml/1²/₃ oz. raspberry vodka**

**20 ml/²/₃ oz. freshly squeezed lime juice**

**chilled soda water, to top up**

**a lime wedge, to garnish**

*Serves 1*

Gently muddle 5 of the raspberries in the bottom of a highball glass. Fill the glass with cracked ice, add the vodka and lime juice and top up with soda water. Stir gently, garnish with a lime wedge and the remaining raspberry and serve.

# Blackberry Basil Mojito

A TWIST ON A MOJITO, THIS FRAGRANT COCKTAIL REPLACES THE RUM WITH VODKA AND THE MINT WITH FRESH BASIL.

**4 fresh basil leaves**

**6 fresh blackberries**

**45 ml/1½ oz. vodka**

**lemon soda, such as San Pellegrino Limonata, to top up**

**a small sprig of fresh basil, to garnish**

*Serves 1*

Put the basil leaves and 4 blackberries in the bottom of a rocks glass and gently muddle. Half fill the glass with cracked ice, add the vodka and stir, top up with lemon soda and stir again. Garnish with the remaining 2 blackberries and a small sprig of basil leaves and serve.

# Berry Caipiroska

THIS TWIST ON THE BRAZILIAN CAIPIRINHA USES VODKA
INSTEAD OF CACHAÇA. IF LIKED, OMIT THE BERRIES AND ADD
EXTRA LIME FOR A CITRUSSY DRINK, CLOSER TO THE ORIGINAL.

**5–7 mixed fresh red berries (depending on their size), plus extra to garnish (choose from strawberries, raspberries and/or blueberries)**

**4 lime wedges**

**2 sugar cubes (brown or white)**

**50 ml/1²/₃ oz. vodka**

*Serves 1*

Put the berries and 3 lime wedges in a rocks glass with the sugar cubes and muddle until the sugar has dissolved and the fruit has released its juices. Top up the glass with crushed ice, pour over the vodka and stir gently to mix and then cap with more crushed ice. Garnish with a few berries and the remaining lime wedge and serve.

# The Black Rose

THIS IS PLEASINGLY TART AND FRUITY, THANKS TO THE
COMBINATION OF A ROSÉ WINE FLOATED OVER MUDDLED
BLACKBERRIES AND FINISHED WITH A SPLASH OF VODKA.

**5 fresh blackberries**

**1 sugar cube (brown or white)**

**freshly squeezed juice of 1 lime**

**20 ml/²/₃ oz. vodka**

**100 ml/3¹/₃ oz. fruity rosé wine**

**a lime slice, to garnish**

*Serves 1*

Put 4 blackberries and the sugar cube in a rocks glass and muddle until the berries are crushed and the sugar dissolved. Add the lime juice, top up the glass with crushed ice and pour over the vodka and wine. Garnish with the remaining blackberry and a lime slice and serve.

# Mediterranean Sparkle

THE FRESH SCENTS OF CITRUS AND MINT COMBINE TO MAKE THIS SPARKLING COCKTAIL THE PERFECT TIPPLE FOR SUMMER.

4 fresh mint leaves

45 ml/1½ oz. vodka

25 ml/¾ oz. triple sec

25 ml/¾ oz. freshly squeezed lemon juice

1 tsp sugar syrup

chilled Cava, or other sparkling white wine, to top up

*Serves 1*

Put 3 mint leaves in a cocktail shaker and muddle gently (do not bruise as this will make the drink bitter). Pour in the vodka, triple sec, lemon juice and sugar syrup. Add a handful of ice cubes and shake until frosted. Strain into a flute and top up with Cava. Garnish with the remaining mint leaf and serve.

# Ouzo Sunrise

BE TRANSPORTED TO A GREEK ISLAND PARADISE WITH THIS UNUSUAL COCKTAIL. THE OUZO ADDS JUST A HINT OF ANISEED THAT PAIRS PERFECTLY WITH THE ORANGE JUICE.

45 ml/1½ oz. vodka

10 ml/⅓ oz. ouzo (Greek aniseed liqueur)

30 ml/1 oz. freshly squeezed orange juice, strained

1 tsp sugar syrup

chilled soda water, to top up

an orange zest, to garnish

*Serves 1*

Add the vodka, ouzo, orange juice and sugar syrup to a cocktail shaker filled with ice cubes. Shake until chilled and strain into a highball glass filled with fresh ice. Top up with chilled soda to taste, garnish with an orange zest and serve.

# AFTER DARK

# Turkish Martini

THIS DRINK IS PURE INDULGENCE. THE SWEETNESS OF THE CRÈME DE CACAO LIQUEUR COMBINES WITH THE FRAGRANT ROSE WATER TO CREATE A TRULY TURKISH DELIGHT.

**cocoa powder, to rim the glass**

**50 ml/1²/₃ oz. vodka**

**1 tsp white crème de cacao**

**2 dashes of rosewater**

**candied rhubarb ribbons, to garnish (optional)**

### Serves 1

Dust a plate with cocoa powder. Wet the rim of a chilled Martini glass and dip it in the cocoa to rim. Add all the remaining ingredients to a cocktail shaker filled with ice cubes and shake well. Strain into the prepared glass, garnish with a candied rhubarb ribbon (if liked) and serve.

# Black Russian

BLACK AND WHITE RUSSIANS ARE CLASSICS THAT HAVE BEEN ON THE COCKTAIL SCENE FOR MANY YEARS. THEY MAKE STYLISH AFTER-DINNER DRINKS WITH THEIR SWEET COFFEE FLAVOUR, WHICH IS SHARPENED BY THE VODKA.

50 ml/1²/₃ oz. vodka
25 ml/³/₄ oz. Kahlúa (coffee liqueur)
a stemmed cocktail cherry,
  to garnish

*Serves 1*

Combine the vodka and Kahlúa in a mixing glass with a handful of ice cubes. Stir to chill and strain into a rocks glass filled with fresh ice cubes. Garnish with a stemmed cherry and serve.

# White Russian

THE WHITE RUSSIAN, WITH ITS ADDITION OF THE CREAM FLOAT, IS GREAT SERVED AS AN INDULGENT NIGHTCAP.

50 ml/1²/₃ oz. vodka
25 ml/³/₄ oz. Kahlúa (coffee liqueur)
25 ml/³/₄ oz. single/light cream,
  chilled
a stemmed cocktail cherry, to garnish

*Serves 1*

Simply make a Black Russian (see above) then layer the chilled cream into the glass over the back of a long-handled barspoon. Garnish with a stemmed cherry and serve.

# Espresso Martini

USE GOOD FRESHLY BREWED COFFEE AND YOU'LL BE
REWARDED WITH A FOAMY HEAD ON THIS MODERN CLASSIC.

25 ml/$^3$/$_4$ oz. freshly brewed strong
  espresso coffee

50 ml/1$^2$/$_3$ oz. vodka

25 ml/$^3$/$_4$ oz. Kahlúa or Tia Maria
  (coffee liqueurs)

$^1$/$_2$ tbsp sugar syrup

3 coffee beans, to garnish (optional)

*Serves 1*

Pour all the ingredients into a cocktail
shaker filled with ice cubes and shake
vigorously. Strain into a Martini glass.
Wait for the cocktail to 'separate' – a
foam will rise to the top and the liquid
below will become clearer. Garnish
with coffee beans (if liked) and serve.

# Almond Espresso Martini

THIS VARIATION IS COMPOSED OF AMARETTO AND VODKA
AS WELL AS A COFFEE LIQUEUR.

25 ml/$^3$/$_4$ oz. freshly brewed strong
  espresso coffee

35 ml/1$^1$/$_4$ oz. vodka

20 ml/$^2$/$_3$ oz. Amaretto Disaronno
  (almond liqueur)

15 ml/$^1$/$_2$ oz. Kahlúa or Tia Maria
  (coffee liqueurs)

3 coffee beans and a pinch of
  toasted, flaked/slivered almonds,
  to garnish (optional)

*Serves 1*

Pour all the ingredients into a cocktail
shaker filled with ice cubes and shake
vigorously. Strain into a Martini glass.
Wait for the cocktail to 'separate' – a
foam will rise to the top and the liquid
below will become clearer. Garnish
with the coffee beans and almonds
(if liked) and serve.

# Chocatini

A DELICIOUSLY RICH DESSERT COCKTAIL, STRICTLY FOR CHOCOLATE LOVERS AND DESIGNED TO BE SIPPED SLOWLY.

90 ml/3 oz. Bailey's Irish Cream Liqueur

30 ml/1 oz. dark crème de cacao

15 ml/$\frac{1}{2}$ oz. vodka

dark chocolate shavings,
   to garnish

## Serves 1

Pour all the ingredients into
a cocktail shaker, add a handful
of ice cubes and shake until
frosted. Strain into a chilled
Martini glass, sprinkle with
dark chocolate shavings
and serve.

# Queen of Tarts

WITH ITS ADVENTUROUS FLAVOUR, THIS STRAWBERRY AND BALSAMIC VINEGAR CONVERSATION-STARTER IS THE PERFECT ICE BREAKER TO SERVE AT A COCKTAIL PARTY.

5 ripe fresh strawberries, hulled
75 ml/2½ oz. vodka
15 ml/½ oz. sugar syrup
5 ml/1 tsp good aged balsamic vinegar
edible flower, such as viola,
    to garnish (optional)

*Serves 1*

Put 4 of the strawberries in a cocktail shaker and muddle to a pulp. Pour in all the remaining ingredients and add a handful of ice cubes. Shake well and strain into a coupe. Garnish with the remaining strawberry on a pick and an edible flower (if liked) and serve

# Babycakes

LOOK NO FURTHER FOR THE ULTIMATE VALENTINE'S COCKTAIL. WHAT COULD BE MORE ROMANTIC THAN SIPPING THESE DELICATELY PERFUMED SPARKLERS TOGETHER.

15 ml/½ oz. vodka
20 ml/⅔ oz. crème de fraise de bois
    (or other strawberry liqueur)
½–1 tsp rosewater, to taste
chilled Asti Spumante or other
    semi-sweet sparkling wine
edible rose petal or other flower,
    to garnish (optional)

*Serves 1*

Pour the first 4 ingredients into a mixing glass, add ice cubes and stir well to chill. Strain into a chilled flute glass and top up with Asti Spumante. Garnish with a petal or flower (if liked), and serve.

# Blood Martini

THIS DRAMATIC-LOOKING RED COCKTAIL IS A FUN CHOICE FOR HALLOWEEN. CAMPARI IS A KEY INGREDIENT IN THE ICONIC GIN-BASED NEGRONI. TO MAKE A NEGROSKI, SIMPLY MIX EQUAL PARTS CAMPARI, VODKA AND SWEET VERMOUTH.

50 ml/1²/₃ oz. vodka

15 ml/¹/₂ oz. Campari

10 ml/¹/₃ oz. crème de framboise (raspberry liqueur)

1 tsp freshly squeezed lime juice

30 ml/1 oz. cranberry juice

a dash of triple sec

a flamed orange zest, to garnish (see NOTE)

## Serves 1

Add all the ingredients to a cocktail shaker filled with ice cubes, shake sharply and strain into a chilled Martini glass. Garnish with a flamed orange peel and serve.

NOTE: To add a flamed orange zest, squeeze the citrus oils from a large strip of orange zest, while holding it skin downwards over a flame, set above the cocktail. Rub the rim of glass with the flamed orange zest before dropping it into the drink (or using it to garnish).

# Gotham Martini

THIS COCKTAIL IS AS SINISTER AND MYSTERIOUS AS ITS NAME
SUGGESTS... TRY VARYING THE AMOUNT OF BLACK SAMBUCA
FOR A DARKER, EVEN MORE THRILLING RESULT.

**60 ml/2 oz. frozen Stolichnaya vodka**
**a dash of black Sambuca**

*Serves 1*

Pour the frozen vodka into a
chilled Martini glass, gently add
the Sambuca and serve.

# Silver Streak

KÜMMEL IS ONE OF THE LEAST FREQUENTLY
USED LIQUEURS IN COCKTAILS, MORE'S THE PITY.
IT HAS A DISTINCTIVE, ALMOST ANISEED-LIKE TASTE
THAT COMES FROM THE CARAWAY SEEDS USED IN ITS
PRODUCTION, AND AS AN ADDED BONUS IT PROMOTES
GOOD DIGESTION. ENJOY THIS AS THE PERFECT
AFTER-DINNER NIGHTCAP.

**25 ml/1 oz. chilled vodka**
**25 ml/1 oz. Kümmel Liqueur**

*Serves 1*

Pour the vodka into a rocks
glass filled with ice cubes.
Add the Kümmel, stir gently
to chill and serve.